Humorous
Funny
Comedy
Solo
Acting
Monologue
Scripts

By
D. M. Larson

TABLE OF CONTENTS

TIPS FOR FINDING MONOLOGUES

1. Be sure to find a monologue that is right for your age. For example, don't pick one about a mother, father, wife or husband if you're not old enough to be one.

2. Select a monologue you can relate to. Find one that has an experience you share or an emotional you can connect to. Look for a character you understand or that is similar to yourself.

THE BIG BAD WOLF
monologue from the play
"Holka Polka"
ISBN-13: 978-1502445490

WOLF

I know exactly what you mean. People misconwhattionize me all the time.

Man, you accidentally knock down some pig's house with a sneeze and they start telling stories about you. And now there's this little girl and her red hood. Who knows what they'll say about this one.

I have self-a-team issues too.

Everyone is always going around saying "what a big nose you have" and "what big teeth you have." It hurts.

I just want to go away some place where I won't bother anyone.

They're always promising happy endings but where's my happy ending? All that happily ever after seems to be reserved for princesses and cute little animals. Especially bunnies. Why are rabbits always getting happy endings?

They're rodents, I tell you. Rodents!

END OF MONOLOGUE

BIG ZERO
(aka The Athletic Supporter)
monologue for male from the play
"The Ghosts of Detention"
ISBN-13: 978-1499111309

(Someone runs out in local team colors and a big "O" painted on his chest [or stomach]. A sports jersey with a big O can work as well. He can have one of those giant foam hands that he waves around. He is excited and screams as he runs on the stage:)

BIFF

Go team! Yeah!!!!!

(He calms down and smiles at the audience)

Was that good? I'm practicing for the big game.

(He looks at his O on his chest)

No, I'm not a zero. I am the 0 in go team. Maybe I am a zero to some people.
But this is my life. This is something that matters to me. Matters to me more than most anything. You know why? Unlike most things, there is a clear start and finish. There are heroes and villains. Winners and losers. There's no pretenders or double agents or false friends. The uniforms make it clear and simple. We know who to root for and who to trust. If only life were this simple... This easy... good and bad... Right and wrong.
What if war could be settled with a game? All the world problems - solved on a Sunday. Once a year we can have China vs USA... India vs Pakistan... Winner gets what they want for a year. No more bombs and no more guns... Just helmets and balls. It sure would be a lot better than what happens now. Because everyone who fights a war is just a big zero.

END OF MONOLOGUE

BLESSING IN DISGUISE
monologue for female
from the scene "Blinded by the Knight"
in the play
"Between Good and Evil"
ISBN-13: 978-1502982308

ASHLEY

It's nice having a guy around who is so helpful. I could get used to having someone who does things for me like this. I don't mean like a servant but as my special little helper.

Especially if I'm blind now... you think I'll be blind forever? I wonder if they have Miss Blind USA? Or maybe I'd be a shoe-in for Miss America if I'm blind. So this could be a blessing in disguise.

You could be up there on stage with me guiding me around... I wonder if that's against the rules?

I could get a cute little guide dog. People love animals too. A blind girl with a dog. I'd win for sure.

Still haven't found my purse? I wonder where it went to.

I hope Joe didn't take it. I have no clue why he would but you never know.

You're such a good listener. I like that. Most the guys I hang out with just want to talk about themselves. They love talking about their bodies and their muscles and how they work out all the time or how they won the big game doing a touch basket or a win down or some such stupidity. Don't you hate it when someone always talks about themselves non-stop?

END OF MONOLOGUE

BONES THE PIRATE GIRL
monologue from female
from "The Pirate and the Princess"
ISBN-13: 978-1515169765

BONES

I am sick of being at sea. I want to feel solid ground. Oh... To take a nice warm bath... Instead of washing in freezing cold sea water. You see what the sea has done to my hair!

(Removes hat or bandana to reveal a mess).

No more pirate's life for me. No more yo ho with these yo-yos. I am tired of all the bottles and bums. I want to drink from a chilled glass goblet... And have some ice cold milk. Fresh cool milk... and ice... a glass of ice water would even be nice. And you know what else you get when you mix milk and ice... this incredible thing called ice cream. You'll never find that on a pirate ship. I'd give anything for a scoop. But you'll never find anything like that on this rust bucket... no milk, no ice cream, not even an itty bitty ice cube... How come the most wonderful things in life spoil so quickly?

END OF MONOLOGUE

BUG-EYED CREATURE
monologue for male
from the play "Bullied, Bungled and Botched"
ISBN-13: 978-1518661082

LUKE

Being the new kid at school is like discovering a new planet. Everything is strange and confusing and you're the weird alien everyone is afraid of - well not fear - you are the gross bugged eyed creature that's completely misunderstood.

(LUKE speaks like an alien to someone passing)

"I come in peace." Ignored as usual. Maybe I have on my cloaking device? No one seems to see me.

(He tries talking to more people as they pass and does the related hand motions for the following [ie Star Trek, Mork and Mindy])

Live long and prosper! Nano nano! Those are my geek gang signs.

May the force be with you. How come that one doesn't have a hand sign? It really needs one.

(He tries out different hand and arm motions)

May the force be with you... may the force be with you... may the force make you live long and prosper. I like that. I need to make a t-shirt with that on there.

You know, the principal made me change my shirt. I had one with Spock doing the Vulcan hand signs saying "Go Trek Yourself" Like anyone could be offended by that. He said students are not allowed to wear anything with words on it. Isn't that ironic? A school banning words.

School is not the place to be unique or stand out. They have this mold they want everyone to fit into. If you're not a certain way the whole school says you're not their type and they reject you.

LUKE (CONT.)

Rejection - life is all about rejection. I am proud to say I have always been the last to be picked for any school activity. Especially when it's sports. I try to make sure I'm last - and if I am really lucky they have too many team members so I have so sit out. To make sure I am last to be picked I always limp so they think I am a liability - and if they don't notice the limp, I add in a nose pick because who wants to pass the ball to a nose picker? Oh, that's a good idea for a hand sign.

(LUKE picks his nose and holds out his finger)

May the force be with you.

(Laughs)

They noticed that one. I know that's gross but hey, I have my bug-eyed creature reputation to maintain.

END OF MONOLOGUE

CALL ME DUMPER
(male version)
from the play "Bullied, Bungled and Botched"
ISBN-13: 978-1518661082

They call me Dumper. I got the nickname when I was a young in' I was watching that Bambi movie. Every time I would see Thumper I would get so excited I would take a dump in my pants. I loved that rabbit for some reason. He just made me so happy. So happy I'd mess myself. We all need something like that in our lives. Something that makes us so happy we lose control. When ma finally got me potty trained, she didn't let me watch that movie anymore.

So I had to find other things to make me happy. Not much did after that. No toy or treat made me as excited as that cute little bunny did.

Maybe I will buy myself a pet bunny rabbit. I will hug and squeeze him and name him George. Bunnies are so soft and cuddly. I just wanna pick them up and smoosh them on my face.

Oh man. I have to go to the crapper just thinking about it.

END OF MONOLOGUE

CALL ME DUMPER
(female version)
from the play "Bullied, Bungled and Botched"
ISBN-13: 978-1518661082

LANE

They call me Dumper. I got the nickname when I was a youngin'... I was watching that Bambi movie. Every time I would see Thumper I would get so excited I would take a dump in my pants. I loved that rabbit for some reason. He just made me so happy. So happy I'd mess myself. We all need something like that in our lives. Something that makes us so happy we lose control. When ma finally got me potty trained, she didn't let me watch it anymore. So I had to find other things to make me happy. Not much did after that. No dolly or sweetie made me that excited. No boy could either. When I got old enough to like boys that is. They ain't worth nothing around here. Boys here never could make me happy and I didn't want to make them happy the way they wanted me to. I tried dating them some but it never works out. There ain't plenty more fish in this sea. These is shallow waters and there are pretty slim pickins. Seems like half of them are my cousins and I am not the kissing cousin type. And the ones left over after that are the catch and release kind. Because when you get one, you quickly want to throw them back. So when I started breaking up with guys my nickname came back to haunt me. All the boys started calling me Dumper again. That's the problem with a small town... things stick around from your childhood. You get a reputation and you get stuck with it. Everyone sees you one way and there's no way out. I could become the smartest, prettiest girl in town and everyone would still call me Dumper. I could go off and feed African kids and cure Ebola and win the Nobel peace prize and come home and they'd still call me Dumper. Why? Because it's easier I guess. Easier to keep you in your place. That way no one gets out of hand or too important. Know your place and play your part.

END OF MONOLOGUE

CASSANDRA
monologue for female
Adapted from the Hysterical History of the Trojan War
ISBN-13: 978-1452871448

CASSANDRA

Don't bring Helen inside, Paris. She will only bring doom on our city. Dooooom! Dooooooooooom!

(She sighs)

How come nobody ever listens to me?

(She hears someone laughing)

Apollo? Is that you? Get over here. I thought you gave me the power to see the future? But nobody listens to me. And now I see the walls of Troy falling down. And no one will listen to me about that either.

(She pauses and listens.)

Fine print? What fine print?

(She pulls a scroll from her pocket)

I can't read this. It's a bunch of drawings. It's all Greek to me.

(She listens)

What? It says that?! How could you do this to me? You gods think you're so smart. Well, I know what happens to you. And I'm not telling. See you, never, Apollo,

END OF MONOLOGUE

CATCHICK
monologue for female
from the play "Between Good and Evil"
ISBN-13: 978-1502982308

CATCHICK

I am tired of my catlike mutant powers. You know how annoying it is to be like a cat? Look. I want to be able to go the beach without getting the urge to use the bathroom. I want to go swimming again. I am tired of all those naps. Please doctor. Take me next.

(Starts choking on something)

And I'm tired of all the hairballs! You can have my powers. Please take them from me. I want to be normal.

END OF MONOLOGUE

COLD AND SHIVERY
monologue for male
from the play "Losers in Love"
ISBN: 9781549653186

RANDY

I saw it! A ghost! Upstairs! I did. It was floating around all spooky like. I think it touched me. I got all cold and shivery. I wanted to scream but when I opened my mouth all I could manage was a little squeak. I was frozen with fear. I thought it was gonna eat my brains or something. Oh, wait. That's zombies, ain't it? Well, it was gonna do whatever ghosts do to me. I could feel it doing something... something real creepy like. You wanna go see it? Or are you too scared? You ain't as brave as me.

(Looks down)

Hey! No, I did not! I spilled a drink on myself, okay? I am not a liar! You go up there and see for yourself. Up there is an honest to goodness, real scary, ghost. I may have lived to tell about it. Will you?!

END OF MONOLOGUE

DEAR GOD
monologue for male or female
from the play "Secrets of My Soul"
ISBN-13: 978-1493533589

(BILLY is an adult who exhibits child-like behavior. He gathers a notepad and goes to get a pencil and sharpens it with a small hand sharpener)

BILLY

A pencil has to be just right. Never too sharp, never too dull. If it's too sharp it might poke me and I'll get lead poisoning and die!I saw a show about that once. People dying of lead... oh, yes and going nuts. I seem to remember Van Gogh got so much lead poisoning he cut off his ear! Ouch! That's like out of Shakespeare... friends, Romans, countrymen! Lend me your ears! Ha!

(Checking the pencil. Pokes him)

Ouch! Too sharp...

(Tosses the pencil. Starts on another)

Now let's try to be a bit dull... dullness has its merits. You can't get hurt. People don't expect as much from you. You do the job, but never for too long.

(Checks pencil. Smiles)

Dull it is.

(Sits with pad and paper)

Now, we're ready.

(Pauses as if listening to someone)
I know, I know... I will address it to Mr. God. You've nagged me a million times about this. I know! Just, just give me time okay.This is an important letter so I don't want to rush it, okay.

(Starts to write)

BILLY (CONT.)

Dear God, I seem to have found something that is yours. A few nights ago, I was in bed, sleeping I think, and then she was there. She was at my bedside, all white and glowing, rocking in my grannie's old chair. I couldn't really look at her though. She was all bright like the sun, giving me those spots on my eyes, those ones you have to blink away until their gone. I must say I was a bit scared and threw the covers over my head. When I looked again, she was still there! I couldn't believe it. I said, "You're hurting my eyes." Kind of a silly thing to say. Why didn't I say, "Are you a ghost?" or something a bit smarter? She said she was sorry and vanished. I was worried I'd licked a few too many pencils and was going to cut off my ear, but then I heard her voice.She told me how she had fallen and couldn't get back home. Her wings were broken and she couldn't fly. "Are you an angel?" I asked her. She said she was. I told her she could stay. See, I don't have many people here, just Mom. I thought she could hang out with me. She said yes, but now Mom wants her to go away. She said it's not good for me to be talking to her. I thought mom liked angels but I guess not. Anyway... can you send a car around or a winged chariot or something to pick her up? She wants to come home now. Sincerely, Billy Graham.

(Giggles)

I wonder if God will know which Billy Graham is writing him? I bet it will get his attention, that's for sure.

(Looks at letter)

Now how do I send this? Does God have a P.O. box? Is it like Santa Clause... you know, Santa, North Pole... God, Heaven...

(Listens to voice)

What? Burn the letter? Why? Will that work? If you say so.

(Goes to a cabinet)

Mom hides the matches from me. They're over here.

(Pulls out box of matches)

BILLY (CONT.)

I think there's a reason she does.

(Gets out an ashtray)

I got this from Motel 6. Nice huh? I collect these things. Every time Grampa used to take me somewhere, I'd get one. No, they're free. They have all kinds of free stuff in motel rooms: pens, notepads, and towels. Grampa liked it all. He said he always wanted to get his money's worth.

END OF MONOLOGUE

DEATH BY DOLLARS
Monologue for male from
"My William Shatner Man Crush"
ISBN-13: 978-1505910155

RANDY

Do you ever get winded putting on your shoes? That's me.. I do. I'm fatty McFat Fat. I got super sized at Mickey D's, crowned at BK and supremed at the Bell. I am the all American consumer, consumed by convenience.

I blame them... I do... They make it too easy... And cheap. That's me. Cheap and easy. I am a dollar menu fanatic. I will eat anything for a buck. That's my motto.

But is it death by dollars? I wonder if the dollar menus are killing me?

But who can afford to eat right? I went in to one of them healthy places once. The cheapest thing in there was a grilled cheese sandwich and they wanted $5 for it! $5 for a grilled cheese! Maybe I could make super healthy pb and j's and sell them outside them ripoff restaurants...

(Calling out to invisible customers)

Gourmet super healthy pbj for $4! And that $4 would get me a dollar menu feast.... Spicy chicken burger... fries... ice cold cola... and some pie. Dollar menu heaven. I'm getting kind of hungry. Gonna get me a spicy chicken sandwich while they last.

(Starts to rush but gets winded and grabs chest)

If yesterday's $1 nuggets don't do me in on the way there.

END OF MONOLOGUE

DOWN THE DRAIN
monologue for male
from the play "A Little Private Education"
ISBN-13: 978-1532853111

(LUKE has called a plumber who has just arrived at LUKE's school. LUKE explains what is going on to him)

LUKE

Today was science day. We were doing experiments and some of my students decided to find out how many paper clips it takes to plug a toilet. I didn't know about it. They took turns in there. I thought they were doing what people normally do in bathrooms. Look. Are you going to fix it or not? I had to do the emergency rate. Nobody could come for a week otherwise.

(Realizes)

The toilet? It's right through there. Enjoy. No, actually it's a nuclear test site. Couldn't you tell? Look at this place. The kids destroyed it. A whole summer of research and idealism out the window...

(fake laugh)

Oh, very funny. Yes, it's down the drain.

(fake smile)

Plumber humor, right?

(mad face)

Well, I don't like it. Aren't you supposed to be doing something? I'm paying you by the hour aren't I? Well, I am in a hurry! Get moving will you. I can find cheaper friends on a street corner. Why didn't you bring your tools up with you? Go get them!

(Plumber exits)

Why can't teachers get paid by the hour?

(Gets a calculator)

LUKE (CONT.)
Let's see Mr. Plum the Plumber gets $100 an hour.

(Adds up)

If I got that for eights hours of school, along with two hours of planning and correcting papers a night. Add some hours for parent teacher conferences, science fairs, Christmas plays... $216,000. Not bad. Maybe we should let big business run education after all.

END OF MONOLOGUE

DUMMY
monologue for male
from "When Mel Fell for Nell"
ISBN-13: 978-1512007183

MEL

This is not me.

(Points to self.)

This is me over here.

(Points to dummy)

He can't say the right thing so I have to speak for him. You know those people who always say the wrong thing at the worst moment in the worst possible way? Well that's me... Well, him... Us... We. Not the royal we either.

(Turns to dummy like he said something)

Babbling? Yes... Thanks dummy... I will get to the point. I didn't mean to stop talking to you... I didn't mean to turn in to him over there... But I just wanted to stop ... Stop before I did any more damage. It feels like my words cause so much destruction. It's like a flower in the wind. You love the gentle breeze of my words when I say sweet things to you... You open up yourself and bloom for me in my kindest moments. But the harsh words break you and tear you apart like a storm. My words storm and rage over you like some black cloud raining over us ripping the gentle petals from you. Like a flower caught in a tornado. I want to whisper sweet things again. I want to nourish you and help you grow your beautiful blossom again, but I get so scared ... I become so afraid of what I will do. You deserve kindness... Upon deserve beauty. You deserve loving words. I want that too. But I feel silenced. I feel crippled inside. I feel broken.
There are so many things I want to say to you though. So many wonderful things I feel for you... See in you... Get from you. I feel better because of you. Like you healed me in some way. I felt sick emotionally before I had you in my life. I felt spiritually dead. You brought me back to life, resurrected the spirit inside me, healed me. You're my angel. That's what you are to me. An angel. So delicate. Such a pure spirit. No hardness hiding the goodness and purity. You leave yourself open to me, giving your full self to me, hiding nothing. You give everything to me... And keep nothing for yourself. You give me your wings so I can fly. You'd remove your heart just to keep mine beating.

You are the greatest gift that has ever been given to me. You complete me. You make me whole. I wish I could speak those words to you.

(Looks at dummy)

I wish this dummy could say what I feel.

END OF MONOLOGUE

EARLY MORNING
monologue for male or female

It's early morning, the time when lovers meet. Enjoying a moment in the warm light of dawn. There's no work for us. No need to slave away indoors. And that's silly when God gave us sunshine to enjoy - by a window - in the sun - with the one you love.

The coffee's brewed – the smell fills the air - so heavenly. We just sit and sniff and soak in the sun and snuggle close.

You look at me with your wild eyes - contemplating love - or some mischief. I get lost in those sapphire eyes, swimming endlessly in blue.

A little pat brings me back. "Play with me" you say with your eyes.

I look and smile and pat you back - all in fun. Eyeing my ear - you lick it.
I lean toward you - it feels so nice. A piece of my fur is stuck on your tongue. I laugh and your ears go back. Now I lick you in kind and you lean in and enjoy the roughness of my tongue as it caresses you.

Early morning. Two cats in the sun. Loving the sun. Loving each other - and - loving everything that isn't dog.

END OF MONOLOGUE

FANNY
monologue for female from
"The Weird, Wild and Wonderful Days of School"
ISBN-13: 978-1482739626

FANNY

News hound? I like the sound of that. The boys at school have always said I've been a dog.

Well, I was walkin' around looking for a story. I went out behind the boys locker room. I always go there hoping to... uh... talk with one of the boys. You know, interview 'em after the big game. And if they ever win a game, I'm gonna get the best darn interview. Losing don't make good news.

Guess what? I heard some of them boys talking in the locker room. They leave the window open cause it gets real hot in there. I don't why cause they ain't got nothing on.

(Hands over a report)
Anyway, I got this. Don't know if it's worth printin.'

You think so? Gosh. You're gonna pay me for it too? Wow. A whole dollar! I feel just like Barbara Walters. I sure look up to her. Her and Jerry Springer.

I will be on the lookout for more stories. I'm headed over to the boys' swimming hole. They got all kinds of interesting things going on over there.

END OF MONOLOGUE

FLOWERS FROM PHIL
monologue for male
from the scene "LOOKS GET IN THE WAY"
in the book "3 Short Comedy Scripts"
ISBN-13: 978-1546726845

(Phil enters a restaurant nervously. He carries a bouquet of flowers. He slowly goes up to a table where his blind date waits. He stops. Turns and leaves again. After a moment he returns. He checks his clothes, drops his flowers, picks them up, gets scared and goes. Then he returns and goes to the table looking nervous but determined)

PHIL

Hey, there, Sidney. I'm early. I mean I'm Phil and I'm early. I am glad you're early too, well, sort of. I was hoping to beat you and get used to the room first. I get nervous in new places. And with new people I get nervous a lot. I brought you flowers. The flowers are a little wilted. They were pretty. I mean there is this wonderful flower shop but I didn't have time to go there today but I did a few days ago and I wanted these flowers. I don't get a date every day you know and I wanted this to be special, so I got the best flowers I know of because I want this to be great. You know what I mean. Well, you probably get a lot of dates. I mean a normal amount of dates, but more than me, but less than say... Madonna. But these flowers were the best... a few days ago.

END OF MONOLOGUE

FOREVER ON HOLD
monologue for female
from the play "When Mel Fell for Nell"
ISBN-13: 978-1512007183

NELL

Doesn't it always seem like we're on hold? We constantly are calling about this or that. We are slaves to the phone, waiting anxiously for a human voice. Companies try to make your experience pleasant by playing music. One company I called even had its own radio station dedicated to entertaining people on hold. My question is, "Why not make that person answer phones too?" There are probably more people working on message systems that put people on hold than there are answering phones. I especially hate the ones that make you feel like you're getting somewhere when you actually aren't. They come up with all these phrases that keep you interested:

(Does a mock answering machine voice)

"Only a few moments more... ring, ring... You have just advanced in our waiting order. Beep. Hello (big pause) you are the next caller. Do not hang up. We will be with you in a moment...after 10 more minutes... We will be with you in a moment. You are the next caller." The most aggravating award goes to the electronic maze of number choices:

(Mock answering machine voice)

"Press one if you need customer assistance. Press two if you need customer information. Press three if you need customer guidance. Press four for more options." You wade endlessly through this maze of choices only to discover you still have to wait an hour to talk to someone.

Then there's the notorious deadline. You wonder, "Did they hang up? Is someone there waiting for you to speak? Did they transfer your call to Albania?" You wait, unsure what to do.

When you finally get to talk to someone, you discover it's not even the right department. They have no clue what you are talking about and transfer you to someone who is equally clueless.

Also while you were waiting they ask you to type in your account number, zip code, date of birth, then when you actually talk to a human, they ask you all over again. THEN WHY DID I JUST TYPE THAT IN!

When talking to a human, we know why it takes so long. They ask you a million useless questions, they find out YOUR question and transfer you to someone who goes through the same things only to discover they have no clue how to help you either!

Finally someone helps you and you end up receiving a six month subscription to Dog's Life Magazine. At least you got something for all your trouble, but wasn't that supposed to be your credit card company?

END OF MONOLOGUE

FUNNY LITTLE FUSSY FACE
monologue for a female
from the play
"Death of an Insurance Salesman"
ISBN-13: 978-1518665547

MINDY

You're so cute when you get mad. You get this funny little fussy face.

(She mocks his mad look)

I started liking you a few years ago.

There was this one meeting we were both at. You had just been promoted and you got up in front of everyone and did this big speech. And every time you looked at me, your eyes stopped on me a moment longer than everyone else. And you'd stumble on your words a little. Maybe it was that low cut shirt I was wearing that day?

Or maybe it was that really short skirt of mine and I was sitting like this.

(She does a sexy sit, crossing her legs in a flirty way)

You're Stuttering. Too cute.

(She suddenly changes her attitude and grows cold, unhappy that she didn't turn him on)

It's not important.

Look... I didn't think it would work out. So I didn't say anything.

Never mind. Forget I Said anything okay?

END OF MONOLOGUE

GIRLS OF AMERICA, BEWARE
monologue for female
from "Blondes Prefer Gentlemen"
ISBN-13: 978-1985331877

DOTTY

You asked me to be on your show and now you cast me aside. It's Hollywood wolves like you that girls have to be careful of these days. You and your empty promises of fame and fortune. "Be on my television program! I'll make you a star!" Promises! Promises! That's all they are. Crazy? You're calling me crazy? There! That proves you're a snake! Calling me crazy in front of millions of viewers! Pretending like you don't know me, like you've never seen me before. Girls of America, beware! Remember this face! Don't let his serpent tongue trick you as it did me!

END OF MONOLOGUE

THE GIRL WHO BROKE HIS FINGER
monologue for female
from "The Ghosts of Detention"

ISBN-13: 978-1499111309

(HARM wears all black and is sharpening a pencil with a pocket knife)

HARM

I don't like to be touched... By anyone... Ever. Touch me and I touch you back... With my fist. I want to hurt them... Cause them pain like they did to me... Suffer... Squirm... Beg for mercy. This guy touched me... with a big smile on his face... Like he did it to be funny... And I broke his finger...

Back in detention again for it... I wonder how long they can keep me in there... I must've racked up a few years by now... At the rate I'm going, I will be 30 before I get out of high school detention.

What's the point of trying... no point in being good and pretending because it never gets me anywhere... I've stopped wishing I'm something, I'm not.

END OF MONOLOGUE

monologue for male or female
adapted from "The Gingerbread Girl"
ISBN-13: 978-1452871448

(FOX sees the Gingerbread Girl approaching and jumps back in fear)

                              FOX
You're... gingerbread!

(FOX moans and holds his tummy)

Oh, I was hoping I'd never see another Gingerbread person ever again.

(FOX sees she is crying)

I'm sorry. Please don't cry. That was a mean thing to say. It's just that I ate the last Gingerbread person to come here and now I have a horrible tummy ache. I wish I could do something about it. It feels like he's a big lump in my stomach that I can't get out.

(If desired, a recording can play or someone off stage can say "Run, run as fast as you can." FOX sighs)

Yes, he's still singing in there too. "Run, run as fast as you can." I can't sleep!

(He cries and whines and then looks at the Gingerbread Girl)

You want to help? But how?

(FOX acts like she grabbed him by the arm and then falls. He acts like he is in the water now drowning)

Help! Help! I can't swim on a full stomach. Oh, oh. Cramp! I'm going down.

(FOX acts like he goes underwater and then comes up again)

Somebody save the fox! I'm going down again. Goodbye cruel world!

(FOX goes down again. Then he pops up one last time)

FOX (CONT.)

Rosebud!

(FOX does a dramatic drowning scene)

END OF MONOLOGUE

GOOD DEEDS AND SUCH
monologue for female
adapted from "Holka Polka"

ISBN-13: 978-1502445490

HILDA

All right, you witches. We've got ourselves a PR problem here. Witches have got a seriously bad reputation here in Fairy Tale Land and it's only getting worse since the Hansel and Gretel incident. I mean, come on people. Eating children. That's just low.

The fairies are thinking of getting rid of all magic. They can and they will unless we turn things around and prove we can handle having it. They gave it to Fairy Tale Land in the first place. And now they want it all back because they think we can't handle it.

We have a crisis here. I mean, what's a witch without her magic? We're nothing, I tell you. Nothing! We'll be just a bunch of creepy old hags with bad hair and skin.

We have to do a major PR thing. Good deeds and stuff. No? Then say "poof" to your magic and learn to use chopsticks because that's all our wands will be good for.

We need to do a good deed. Not just any good deed, but a whopper of a good one. We're going to save the Prince... Aka Sleeping Handsome.

But think of the PR. Witches saving the Prince who has been put under a sleeping spell. And we must do it before some bubble headed princess manages to beat us to it.

END OF MONOLOGUE

GREENIE
(THE LAST LIBERAL)
monologue for female
from "Operation Redneck"
ISBN-13: 978-1540824349

(Tina is a small town girl who is worried about her friend, Julie, bringing her liberal boyfriend to their small conservative town)

TINA

Now wait a minute. You know how narrow minded people here can be.

Well... your Greenie boyfriend doesn't go to church. And Your Grandpa's a minister. Your boyfriend thinks all hunters should be shot. Isn't your dad a big game hunter?

And your boyfriend doesn't want to have any kids. He thinks the Earth is way too overpopulated? Doesn't your Grandmother hold the town record for giving birth to the most kids? They have a picture of her at the maternity ward in town.

This is bad. The last liberal who came to town nearly got themselves killed. Remember when your cousin Earl brought home that girl from California? She had her armpit hair braided! She did! JJ said he saw it. And she chained herself to the local Steak in the Rough BBQ and refused to leave until they served salads. You know what happened to her? She got run over by a garbage truck. Did so, ran right over her foot.

It's not safe for them greenies here. You better tell your boyfriend not to come.

END OF MONOLOGUE

GROWING UP IS HARD TO DO
monologue for male from "Between Good and Evil"
ISBN-13: 978-1502982308

(THAD is under a bedroom sheet. He peeks out nervously. He is in pajamas)

THAD

I feel so strange tonight, waking up in the full moon's light. Something had changed. I am not the same. I'm getting really hairy. More hairy than I thought a man could be. This is rather scary and ...and....my voice is changing toooooo.

(He howls and then slaps his hands over his mouth)

Was that a howl? And my hands... Look at my nails... did I forget to cut them or are they longer... And sharper than before?

(He struggles with the sheet.... He gets all wrapped up in a panic. He claws and rips it)

Claws! Actual claws!

(He finally gets free of the sheet)

Mirror? Where's a mirrorrrrrr!

(Big growl)

Was that a growl? From my stomach? What's there to eat? I could really use some meat.

(Holds his stomach)

Growing up is so hard to do...

(Reaches back And feels something bulging at his rear)

....especially when you're growing a tail toooooooo!

(He howls and holds his bottom and carefully scoots off stage)
END OF MONOLOGUE

HUMPTY DUMPTY PRIVATE EGG HARD-BOILED DETECTIVE
Monologue for male
adapted from the play "Holka Polka"
ISBN-13: 978-1502445490

HUMPTY

It was a dark and stormy night in fairyland. A night just perfect for witches. With fairy godmother in the clink, I began to wonder if we were ready for a world turned topsy-turvy. Sweet witches and friendly wolves. Wise wizards and princesses with pig noses. It's a world gone mad but somehow things are looking sunny-side up and we may find some kind of happily ever after in fairytale land. I was about to call it a day because I had this over easy feeling coming over me... when she rolled in. She had the figure of a fortress and the countenance of a cobra. She was the goddaughter; the witchiest woman west of Walla Walla. I wondered if this was some kind of yolk. I had already cracked the case of the sleeping prince. Fairy godmother was left with egg on her face. The sleeping spell was only the Easter coloring on a much more rotten egg. She had bigger eggs to fry. And the corruption nearly broke fairytale land apart. Thankfully they had me to put it back together again. I could continue walking on eggshells around her like everyone else or I could put all my eggs in one basket and say it straight. I knew she was trouble and I told her so. I told her she was like one of those riddles that scramble your brains like, "what came first, the chicken or the egg?" I told her to beat it unless she wanted to have a talk with all the King's horses and all the King's men. But then her eyes teared up and I was speechless because I'd never seen this cool egg crack before. Hey, I've got feelings. I'm a bit soft-boiled around the dames. And this dame needed help. And help is what I do, because I'm Humpty Dumpty, Private Egg. Hard-boiled detective.

END OF MONOLOGUE

I HATE BUFFETS
monologue for female
from "When Mel Fell for Nell"

ISBN-13: 978-1512007183

NELL

I hate buffets... Not for the obvious like germs... Get your fingers out of there! Yes I know I'm not your momma.... Just do it... That's gross... Don't you dare lick your fingers. Gross... Okay maybe it's the germs too...

But here is my main problem. All you can eat is way too much for me... It's too much for everyone. Why do we need so many options? I hate all these choices. And I always feel like I make the wrong one.

I eat something and it sits like a lump in my stomach... I try another... Two lumps. Another... It's all terrible... Buffets don't give you more... Just a lot of bad choices... I just want to find one place... A great place with something really good. One really good thing I can count on to always be good for me. So yummy I will just eat it over and over again... That one wonderful thing that settles inside me...

(Burps or almost throws up...)

Not this... This torture... Eating and eating bits of everything... Tearing me up inside... It's gonna rip me apart.

END OF MONOLOGUE

I NEED DETENTION
monologue for male
from "The Ghosts of Detention"
ISBN-13: 978-1499111309

JIMMY

I need detention. I really need detention. See, there's this girl... I know, I know, it always starts with a girl ... But this girl is special... I mean it this time... Really special. Her name is Harmony... But she goes by Harm. Cute huh? She can harm me any time she wants. And she has too. A couple of times. But I deserved it... Cause I touched her once. I didn't touch her anywhere bad. Just on the shoulder. And she broke my finger. So I guess we kind of have held hands. I was just gonna ask to borrow a pencil. One of those ones she sharpens with her pocket knife and then throws in the ceiling all over school. She even got one in the gym ceiling. You know how high that is? Like 5000 feet. And I just stand under those pencils, hoping one will fall down and I can have one of them for my very own. Something to remember her by. Until I get in to detention.

I gotta figure out some way to get detention because I wanna see her more... Be with her more... And turn Harm into Harmony again... Cause I see that beautiful harmony under all that black and gloom. She just needs a reason to smile and I want to be that reason.

So I have to get detention. What's something good... I mean I want it to be really really good so I get thrown in there a long time... Plus I have to make it worth it... Something great that she can respect... How about giving the principal a wedgie? That would do it... A good old up the back over the head mega wedgie. Let's do this.

END OF MONOLOGUE

IT'S JUST RIGHT
monologue for male
from "A Little Private Education"
ISBN-13: 978-1532853111

(LUKE runs a private school out of his home and it is paid for by a wealthy woman named Mrs. Poke who is coming to visit him this evening. Mrs. Poke has hinted at wanting to have more than a business relationship with him)

LUKE

(Rushing around. Steps on something)

Aw! Another crayon! I'll never get this place clean. Mrs. Poke will think I'm running a pig stye.

(Steps on another crayon)

Aw! Die evil crayon.

(Stomps crayon to death)

I feel much better now. I hope everything is okay in here. I want it to be comfortable for her.

(Pulls out something from the school)

But I want it to look like a school.

(Pulls out something else from the school)

A really good school.

(Pulls out more)

Now it's a mess again.

(Cleans up)

LUKE (CONT.)

Music. That's what we need.

(Turns on. Tunes. Hard rock)

Too loud.

(Tunes. Easy listening. Dances to it funny)

Ew! Not that.

(Tunes . 70's Disco. Does a Saturday Night Fever impression)

I can feel the polyester already. (Tunes)

There must be something Mrs. Poke would like.

(Tunes. Classical)

Not too loud. Not too soft. Not too suggestive. And to quote that famous philosopher Goldilocks, "It's just right."

(Knock at door)

Here she is. Breathe, Luke, breathe.

(Goes for door)

Coming.

(Opens door. He sees Mrs. Poke who is in a sexy outfit)

Uh… Wow… I mean… Uh… … hi.

END OF MONOLOGUE

KILL FIRST, GLOAT LATER
monologue for male or female
from the play "Between Good and Evil"

ISBN-13: 978-1502982308

(Mezmero, a super villain, stands over a hole in the ground)

MEZMERO

I finally did it. I finally beat you. And all I had to do is NOT reveal my evil plan. Why do we villains always do that? Why do we have this strange need to tell you all our devious plots before we do them? That always gives you time for that last minute save... That last minute effort that gets you through... Or perhaps we reveal some flaw in our plan you are able to exploit. Not this time. This time it was kill first, gloat later. This is so much better. I get to brag now. Bragging is so much better than revealing the plan. Time for a victory dance on your grave!

(Mezmero does a dance around Super Dead Man's hole in the ground)

END OF MONOLOGUE

MASKED MAN

from

"My William Shatner Man Crush"

ISBN-13: 978-1505910155

SADIE

Oh, it was so exciting. It reminded me of my senior prom... Or was it the time the bank was robbed? Either way, it was so exciting.

I have always loved masked men. I enjoy a bit of mystery. Most men are so simple.... Easy to read. But a masked man becomes a whole new kind of man. One with something to hide. A mystery I must uncover.

I miss Roger. He was a mystery. We met one of those costume parties where everyone was wearing a mask. It was his eyes... His beautiful eyes... I could get lost in those eyes forever.
I never told anyone this but I know Roger was the one who robbed that bank. I recognized his eyes. And the way he waved that gun around and yelled at people... It was so scary... And exciting. That's always how he was.... Scary and exciting.

It was so nice seeing Roger again... Rushing on the bus, being a hero. I like him being a hero too. As long as he is in a mask. I love the mask. Good or bad, the mask is perfect.

Please tell him I'm here. That I want to see him again... and give him a kiss.

END OF MONOLOGUE

THE MASTER OF FART ZEN
monologue for male
from "The Weird, Wild and Wonderful Days of School"
ISBN-13: 978-1482739626

(actor will either need to have someone with fart recordings or hide whoopie cushions inside their costume to make the fart noises themselves - or eat a lot of beans and drink a lot of soda first)

MASTER

Please enter. All are welcome here. So what is the source of your tension? Pupils. Assume position... Ichi.

(MASTER gets in a certain position and a slight fart)

We are reaching a state of advanced relaxation. All tension is something that is within you. Stress becomes bottled up and new stress makes it all shaken and builds inside you. If you have to way to relieve that stress, then it grows until it becomes unhealthy and even painful. Position Ni!

(MASTER does a different position and does a slightly better fart)

Is your tension causing you pain? Then you must have a proper way to expel the demon which festers within. Prepare for the next position! Position San!

(MASTER gets in a different position and farts a bit better)

We must all reach a state of perfect relaxation. But only the Fert-zen master can achieve such a perfect state through repeated practice. The goal of all Fert-zen students is to reach position Shi. Prepare for position Shi.

(MASTER gets in an odd position. Long pause. Suddenly the fart comes quietly then builds and gets stronger. The fart grows and lights fade to black. The fart builds and then stops. Then continues after a moment almost explosively. Wait for silence from audience and then a little fart then comes again just to finish it off)

END OF MONOLOGUE

MASTER OF ROCK! SCISSORS! PAPER!
monologue for male from "The Weird, Wild and Wonderful Days of School"
ISBN-13: 978-1482739626

MASTER

You thought the game was rock, scissors, paper. You are wrong! The ancient game has been dishonored by scissors and paper. It is a mockery of the true art of the challenge. Shall I tell you the story? If you wish to hear the story, you must say, "Yes, Master." Now Say... "Pretty please with a cherry blossom on top." Fine. I will tell you the story.

(The master can pull out a scroll or book to help with the story. The book could be a giant popup book.)

It all began with the rock. Not the wrestler.No, the rock was a big fat lazy slob. But he was unmovable. He was a champion sumo wrestler because no one could move him. He won every match. And then he sent a challenge out to all warriors that no one could defeat him. So samurai and ninja from all over Asia came to fight him, but even a sword could not pierce his rock-like skin. But then a magician from a distant land came with a mighty weapon. A firecracker! No one had seen such a huge firecracker before. The magician faced off against the Rock. He lit the fuse and placed it at the Rock's feet. The Rock did not care. He did not think anything could defeat him. Suddenly, there was a huge explosion. There were screams and cries of pain. And when the smoke cleared, the Rock had fallen. Everyone stood quietly and couldn't believe their eyes. A few began to cry. The magician's laugh broke the silence and he pulled another, even bigger firecracker from his robes. The magician yelled, "I shall rid this land of the Rock forever!" He placed the firecracker next to the Rock and lit it. But then a young one, who was a big fan and collected all the Rock memorabilia, sprang into action. He snatched up a sword and "swish", cut the fuse, saving the rock from destruction.

(Master bows)

So I ask that you no longer dishonor the game with scissors and paper.

(Master closes book or scroll and leaves)

END OF MONOLOGUE

MELINDA STREET

monologue for female from "Somebody Famous" ISBN-13: 978-1539753483

Monologue #1

MELINDA

Mind if I step out for a bit, Officer?

Just for a second. I promise I'll be right back.

Oh, what's the mater, Officer? Am I getting a little too close.

Oh, I'm so scared. Little police man's gonna handcuff me. Or is that a game you like to play with the girls?

Monologue #2

MELINDA

Look, ladies. If you want to act with me you've got to follow a few simple rules.

When I'm on stage, you all back up and give me room.

The key is to stay upstage of me at all times.

(Points upstage)

That's upstage. And I will be downstage.

(She wakes downstage regally)

Who is the professional award winning actor here? Me. So let me handle this.

The key, girls, is to not steal my light. You'll have your time to play act while I'm off stage.

(reacts to one of the other women and speaks mockingly)

But... But... Nothing. That's the way it's going to be.

END OF MONOLOGUE

MR. MOO IS MAD
monologue for male
from "Losers in Love"
ISBN: 9781549653186

MR. MOO

You humans have a love hate relationship with us bovine. We are used and abused. We're all shakes and burgers to you aren't we? You can't get enough of us. You even use our cowbells in music! Don't try to deny it. I know you're always wanting more cowbell in your songs.

(Smiles)

Hey, do you know why cows wear bells?

(Pause)

Because their horns don't work.

(Laughs at his own joke)

A little barnyard humor.

(Frowns when he remembers what he was talking about)

But seriously, we have tried to get along with you. We have tried to give you our fair share. What do you give us in return? You take away our fields... You lock us up in fences. You cage us. We no longer can enjoy those long lazy days of grazing in open prairies. Instead we are imprisoned in corrals of corruption. Corporate corruption which feeds on greed and wants to squeeze every drop out of us for a few extra pennies.

(Angry)

How dairy you?! You butter try harder to get along with us or we're cutting you off faster than you can cut the cheese. No, I'm not milking this for all it is worth.

(Gets sad, almost in tears)

MR. MOO (CONT.)

Because it seems like every human is in on it. If it's not corporate hogs then it's those of you who want to protect the prairies and deny us fresh grass to graze upon. Do we too not have a right to be free, to feed openly and enjoy what the Earth provides? Or are we only to give and you only to take?

(Mad again)

We try to get along with you but now you've crossed a line? We're not in mooood anymore. This has gotten udderly ridiculous. I know you're probably going to say something like, "Don't have a cow!" What does that mean anyway?! Well. I'm taking a stand. No more tipping this cow.

(Resolved)

I've decided to be a bully now. I have vowed to steal kids' milk money. We're keeping our milk. We're denying you Double McWhoppers with cheese.

(Grows proud)

You might ask "Where's the beef?" Well, I'm here to tell you it's right here! Cowabunga!

END OF MONOLOGUE

MUGGED IN METROPOLIS
monologue for female
from "Between Good and Evil"
ISBN-13: 978-1502982308

(A woman, Lo, returns from chasing someone and is upset. She's in the town square of Metropolis, Illinois next to the Superman statue)

LO

Hey! Wait a minute! Wh... what?! No! This isn't right! I come to your stupid town and the first thing that happens is that I'm mugged? First guy I meet and he's a con man. Kent the con man. Ah! Why am I so stupid? Don't talk to strangers. (Yells at statue) Isn't that what you teach this kids, Superman? Well, I blew it. Blabbed to some random dude and he mugs me. Why did I follow a dream? I am an idiot. A stupid, dumb bubblehead.

(She plops down on a bench)

I'm always a victim. There's not enough heroes in this world. Not enough Supermans. Sure, there's bunches of you parading around in costumes, but there's not many real men of steel. Not any willing to take a bullet for me.

(She jumps up again)

And you know what?! My life savings was 50 bucks! How's that for irony? And my credit cards are maxed out! Ha! Jokes on you!

(Plops down on bench again)

I just want my lucky key chain back.

END OF MONOLOGUE

MY MASK
monologue for female
from the scene "Looks Get in the Way"
from the book "3 Short Comedy Scripts"

ISBN-13: 978-1546726845

SIDNEY

Wanna see me without my mask?

Don't be nervous. I'm not this scary looking for real.

I'm kind of ugly but nothing like this mask.

Don't worry. I don't have a huge nose or weird teeth or a huge mole on my face. I'm just not very good looking.

You're really nice. You deserve to see my real face. You've passed the test.

END OF MONOLOGUE

MY WILLIAM SHATNER MAN CRUSH
monologue for male
from "My William Shatner Man Crush"
ISBN-13: 978-1505910155

FRANK

Why am I waiting in line with all these losers? I am a grown man... With a job... I don't even live in my parents basement. Yet here I am... Waiting in line to meet William Shatner. I even got here early. I have a sleeping bag... Snacks... I am not even going to explain about the bathroom situation. Why do we put ourselves through this? I have dignity... I have a life... I don't need this. I should walk on out of here and leave this insanity behind me. Shatner once told us to get a life. It's time I got one.

(Then he get excited when he sees William Shatner approach)

There he is!

(Frank squeals with excitement)

He's coming over here! William "frackin'" Shatner is coming over here to meet me.

(Frank looks at a person who is in front of him)

Oh, wow, Mr. Shatner. This is such an honor... Yes sir... First in line to see you. You're my favorite celebrity. Well, my favorite person in the whole world actually. I love everything you've done. Everything is better when you're in it. I love Star Trek, T.J. Hooker, 3rd Rock from the Sun, Miss Congeniality, Boston Legal... even the Priceline commercials... I love you... Meeting you is the most magical moment in my life so far... Thank you, Mr. Shatner... Call you Bill? Oh wow... Bill. Bye bye... Live long and stay awesome!

(Gets really embarrassed and disgusted with himself)

Oh my God! What is wrong with me?! What am I? A fangirl? I need my head checked... Oh, no... I have a man crush, don't I? I have a William Shatner man crush. I want to die now. Crawl under a rock with the other creepy fans... And....

(He notices they are opening the doors at the store he is waiting in line at)

FRANK (CONT.)
They're opening the doors! I am so getting my boots autographed.

(Frank picks up a back with something in it)

Hey Bill! Look what I found on eBay for you to sign! It's the actual rocket boots from Star Trek V!

END OF MONOLOGUE

NEW LOVE FOUND
monologue for male
from "Flowers in the Desert"
ISBN-13: 978-1530169085

LINC

Community service... Better than jail I guess. I just wish I didn't have to wear this stupid uniform. And these sick people... Why is everyone in the hospital so sick all the time? I hope I don't catch anything. And who wants books and magazines anymore? Especially out of date ones. How old are these magazines? "Man on the Moon!" I feel like the man on the moon working in this place, wandering around with my books and magazines and flowers, totally out of place in some weird outer space... Lost on the dark side of the moon. Well, I guess they'd want something to read if the TV in their room is broken. Man, that would suck. Stuck in a hospital bed with no TV. Seems like the only one who wants anything from me is Old Ms. Sadie. I hope she doesn't want me to read to her again. There is nothing creepier than reading a romance to an old lady.

(Sees a new patient)

Wait a minute. Who is that? Check out the new girl. What's her name? Where's the room chart? Shelly... That's a pretty name. I have to meet her... I wonder if she wants a magazine... Teen Beat? No she looks more classy than that... She looks like a Cosmo girl... I mean Cosmo woman. And she looks like all woman under that little gown...

(Looks frantically at cart for something to give her)

Flowers.... I will give her flowers. Old Ms. Sadie has enough flowers ... She doesn't need these. Little note... Lost...

(Takes note off flowers and tosses it)

LINC (CONT.)

New love ... found.

(Boldly goes to meet Shelly)

END OF MONOLOGUE

THE PAPARAZZI FART
monologue for male
from the play "Losers in Love"
ISBN: 9781549653186

RANDY

Have you ever farted in front of a fan? I call it a paparazzi, because farting in front of a fan is like some terrible stalker that follows you and you can't escape. The worst one I've ever done was my first. I had the ultimate silent but deadly gas bomb seep from me. I happened to be standing in front of a fan at the time. The results were glorious. This ultimate gas passing experience was a mix of nerves and a bean burrito, one of those frozen burritos that are made from the cheapest mystery beans ever grown. I wanted to talk to my teacher about something personal and there was only a short time before the whole class would get back from gym. I snuck out early so I could talk to the teacher alone. It was a hot day in May and the teacher had a big fan pointed at the classroom to keep things cool. As I approached, I felt my stomach churn and deposit something painful into my bowels. I bent forward a bit and my teacher looked concerned. I started talking to hide the noise of the gas escaping out of me. At first I was thankful it was silent, but then I realized I was standing in front of the fan and the whole class walked in. The deadliest bottom sewage smell I ever produced oozed from me and filled the air. Students screamed and gasped. Chaos swarmed the room. I looked at the teacher who couldn't tell what was going on since he was on the other side of the fan. The class struggled into their desks with their noses pinched and mouths moaning. I don't even remember what I wanted to talk to my teacher about, but I sure remember that fart. It was glorious.

END OF MONOLOGUE

PEANUT BUTTER FLAVORED TOOTHPASTE
monologue for female
from "Blondes Prefer Gentlemen"

ISBN-13: 978-1985331877

DEBBY

It's such an honor to be auditioning for you. I love all your commercials, like the one about Frank's Flavored Dentures. Hilarious! I need a moment to warm up before we get started. Mi, mi, mi. La, la, la. Okay, I'm ready as a bowl of spaghetti. Here is my audition: "Peace's peanut butter flavored toothpaste. Brush with our better peanut buttery paste." And here is version 2. I thought I'd rewrite it a bit. I hope you don't mind. "Peace's peanut buttery paste is something you should taste. Brush better with Peace's peanut buttery toothpaste." How's that? Was that good? You like it? Did I get the part? Please… I need this job. My rent is overdue and I need this so badly. Or I could be one of your writers… did you like my version better? Please!!!

END OF MONOLOGUE

PEARLS OF WISDOM
monologue for female
from "Secrets of my Soul"
ISBN-13: 978-1493533589

(A young Idaho woman standing and staring with excited fascination. A crib is near a chair behind her. Phrases in quotes are done in voices of herself as younger or as other characters in her life)

TYRANNY

"Oh, my heck!" was all I could say when I first saw him. I'd never seen a man in quite this way before. I'd finally ripened... got my buds and flowered. Boys no longer caught my fancy; I was after a whole hunk of man now. I examined him with a horrific fascination that my mother had warned me about. The church too for that matter.

(Mimicking an old lady)

"Protect your pearls, girls," said Sister Sue as she handed us each a little baggy. The baggy held something like a clamshell. Inside each shell was a little pearl.

(Pretending to be another young girl)

"I wonder if it's real," Jennie Lynn asked wide eyed. I looked at my own pearl dipped in Elmer's glue.

(Speaking as her younger self)

"Not sure," I said as I studied it. "I think you bite it or something to tell. Saw this murder mystery on TV once. They'd made some kind of drug look like pearls. They crushed the pearl necklace with a tea cup and discovered it." Jennie Lynn just gave me a snot nosed upturned look.

(Pause. Reflects as her older self) The meaning of the pearl escaped me until now.

(Mimicking old lady again)

TYRANNY (CONT.)

"Keep that pearl safe. Don't let the boys have your pearl until you're ready," Sister Sue warned. I'm sure she attached some additional meaning to it, like about marriage, but I couldn't quite remember that part. I'd forgotten most the lessons I'd learned in church. Jesus no longer man enough to keep my attention.

(Remembering. Looking longingly ahead)

It was a cowboy that first got my attention. As I stared at this man, I grew hot and anxious. I about threw him my pearl. "Take it, take it, take it!" I chanted in my head. He was nearly close enough to taste. His horse sweaty from a long ride, he stroked it gently. I watched, wishing to be stroked. Then he saw me, his eyes dancing, his half grin giving me shivers.

(Mimicking a Western guy)

"Well, if it ain't my little cousin Tyranny."

(Aside)

Mama had given me that name. Grannie said momma lay there all puzzled to high heaven about what she was gonna call me.

(Mimicking her mom)

"Get me a dictionary," she ordered and thumbed through Webster's til she found a word that sounded nice: Tyranny. She thought it was pretty sounding.

(Pause)

Now where was I? Oh, yeah, my cousin Skeeter.

(Becoming her younger self)

"Hi, Skeeter," I climbed up the side of a stall and straddled it. Skeeter sauntered up and swatted me on the backside.

(Smacks her own rear for effect, then talks like a Western guy)

TYRANNY (CONT.)

"Turning out to be a fine filly, ain't ya?" I blushed, still felt his hand where it had smacked me. I liked it. I wanted him to do it again. Skeeter leaned in close, so close I could have kissed him. His breath like beer and garlic mixed. I could nearly taste it on my lips as I licked them. "You better hold on tight to your pearl or some guy's gonna snatch it away." He smacked my rear again and headed out. I grinned uncontrollably. Please, God, let Skeeter take my pearl.

(Back to older self)

But he never did, though I wish he had. At least my family might still love me then. Then I'd be the victim. This way, I am the bad one. Raped at thirteen by a cousin would have been far more noble in my family's eyes. Sure Skeeter would have been in for it, but at least I'd be okay. You might be thinking that I'm kind of strange thinking that way about my cousin but I know my history. People's been doing this sort of thing for years you know. Look at Egypt. All kinds of those guys married family. In my biology class they talked about royalty marrying family like crazy in England. Though I guess that was kind of bad cause they got this disease. What was it again? Cycle cell ameba? Round here they still think family is okay. Plenty of people find love with a second or third cousin. Sometimes closer. Guys joke that they go to family reunions to meet girls. Mostly they don't, sometimes they do. My cousin Brock has it bad. His parents are related somehow and that's why Brock has fingers for toes and thumbs for fingers. Funniest looking hands you ever saw. We always point at Brock and say, now that's what happens when cousins marry. This ain't nearly as bad as the Eggerstons, distant cousins from a little town in Idaho called Mud Lake. Not too many people there that's not related. Old papa Eggerston has been married a few times. He's proud that his current wife isn't a blood relative; she's just his step-daughter. But previous family encounters had given his family strange hands without fingernails. Bizarre looking worms of hands. I'm like you all and I decided to stay clear of family. I shouldn't have bothered though. I'm worse off now because of it.

(Pause. Goes to crib)

I'd met Buck at a party. I got drunk. Drunk on beer and garlic. I must have eaten ten pizzas that night. Must have had twenty beers. Buck raped me... excuse me... courted me. They don't have date rape in these parts. Here they call it courtship.

(Mimics mother)

59

Sure, momma was a bit annoyed with old Buck. "You don't sleep with sixteen year old girls. You're thirty-one for Christ's sake." Momma gave him two options, marriage or jail. He took the logical course for once in his life and then slipped away.

(Picks up baby from crib)

So here I am, married, with a kid, still with my momma. My husband is somewhere getting some other girl drunk, taking her pearl. One day he may come back. But if he does, God help his pearls, cause I'm gonna cut 'em off. Cut 'em off and mount them like a couple of fish. Hang 'em right next to my team roping trophies and label them "pearls of wisdom." They'll be a warning to any man who tries to take my girl's pearl.

(Strokes babies head)

I often sit here praying all men will die before my baby's old enough. My best hope for her is to be a lesbian. "Don't let them take your pearl, little Ennui." Then I sing to her, singing, hoping she'll remember...

(Sings)

"Hush little baby, don't say a word, Momma's gonna buy you a butcher knife. If that butcher knife won't cut, Momma's gonna hit'm with a pickup truck..."

END OF MONOLOGUE

ACTING TIPS FOR HUMOROUS MONOLOGUES

New actors often ask how they can have more expression in their voices and avoid being monotone. The key is any good monologue performance is to show a variety of emotions.

When you go through a script, think of different emotions the character might be feeling.

Look at the monologue Protecto (Kid Hero). At first he is frustrated. Then he starts to get excited at "I love being a hero." Next he shows anger about a bully at school... "There's this kid at school..." Then he is playful when he talks about school lunch. Excitement builds again when talks about getting a catchphrase. But then at the end he is confused and having second thoughts. You'd want to reflect that in your voice and acting. Show each of those emotions for each part.

Next, look at each sentence. Pick out a word or two in each sentence that you'd want to put the most emphasis on. In the line "I've always dreamed of being a hero." You might pick "dreamed" or "hero" or both. Say these keywords with more strength... say them a little more clearly or forcefully.

PROTECTO (KID HERO)
monologue for male or female
from "Between Good and Evil"
ISBN-13: 978-1502982308

PROTECTO

I've always dreamed of being a hero. I've tried everything to become super. I let a spider bite me... no spider powers; just lots of itching. I tried standing too close to the microwave oven hoping the radiation would change me. Nothing. And I got in trouble for making so many bags of popcorn. But I took it all to school and had a popcorn party. I was a hero that day. So I guess it kinda worked. I love being a hero. I love helping people. I love making them happy. And I hate bad guys. I hate creeps who hurt people. There's this kid at school... he is always hurting everyone. I am sick of him hurting us. I just need those super powers. I need something that will make him stop.

(Lost in thought)

Maybe if I eat more of the school lunches. They look radioactive. If I get enough green hotdogs and brown ketchup in me... something is bound to happen.

(Nods in approval)

And I need a catch phrase like "gonna smoosh me a baddie"... and a cool costume... actually last time I was in the bathroom, I saw the perfect superhero name. Protecto! Instead of a telephone booth like superman, I could use a bathroom stall and those Protecto seat covers could be a cape... and make a toilet paper mask. Nothing scares bad guys more than bathroom stuff.

(Thinks then frowns)

Or maybe it will really make them want to give me a swirly. I better rethink this.

THE END or how they say in the comics... EXCELSIOR!

SCHOOL NEWSPAPER
monologue for female
from "The Weird, Wild and Wonderful Days of School"
ISBN-13: 978-1482739626

(BULA looks through the paperwork on her desk at the school newspaper office)

BULA

Now let's see. What do we have for next week's top story? Looks like we're down to two: Where is the school nurse sneaking off to during the day? Or who are the imaginary people the principal is always talking to? Wow. Where do we ever get such good news? I'll bet no other school paper can boast about these kind of headlines.

What else we got?

Let's see what Fanny brought me. Oh! This will do fine on the society page. Romance is a budding at the school. This week Jimmy Joe Johnson's heart is a palpitating for none other than Betty Sue Mall. Unfortunately he's feeling a bit shy and can't figure out a way to tell Betty he's got those special feelings for her. Don't you worry, though, Jimmy. She'll know all about it soon enough. Best wishes to both of you in this new found romance.

Very nice. Now where's the school crime report? Here we go.

Crime wave hits the halls of our school. Hide your valuables. Monte the Hall Monitor says we had a record number of incidents this week. He caught one group of kids playing with firecrackers and trying to blow up the chemistry lab. He wrote over ten tickets for excessive farting in the gym. And he rescued some guy from a locker that his girlfriend had stuffed in him. He must have done something pretty bad. Girl power gone wild. This school is out of control.

END OF MONOLOGUE

SIMPLE, TRUE, HONEST LOVE
monologue for female
from the scene "Princess from Another Planet"
from the book "Between Good and Evil"
ISBN-13: 978-1502982308

(Lila is from Earth and is the girlfriend of Peter, a scientist, who has been asked by an alien Princess to come to her planet to help with a crisis. Lila doesn't trust the alien Princess and wants to stop Peter from going with her)

LILA

I don't care. I won't let you take Peter from me. I'll risk everything to save him. He's my world. I don't need anything else but him.

(To Peter)

Quiet. You're in trouble too mister. Let's go, Peter.

(Peter seems torn and hesitates)

I know I'm not perfect, but I do really love you. She's just going to use you. Chew you up, take what you have to offer and then spit you out. You are just a tool to her. A means to an end and then she'll cast you aside. You know I'm not like that. You know I love you for you and not what I can get out of you. So... what do you chose? A crazy, wild fling that will end in ruin... or simple, true, honest love?

END OF MONOLOGUE

SLEEPING SPELL
monologue for female
from "Sleeping Handsome"

MORGAN

So Prince Charles. It looks like we're getting engaged! It's about time the witch gets to be the princess. I'm tired of all those cutesy chicks getting their happy endings. Time for the bad girls to get theirs...

(Does a dance)

Uh huh.. That's right. You dig it?

(Reacts to Prince)

What do you mean I am disqualified. I won your riddle contest. What ugly clause in the rules? Let me see that.

(Grabs scroll)

This is horrible. I didn't know about this. Oh, I hate the fine print. You should be ashamed at having a rule like this. That's so... Evil.

(Evil grin)

I knew I liked you.

Well... You want ugly? I'll show you ugly. You haven't seen anything yet.

(She pulls out her magic wand and waves it)

Here's a nice spell who will make girls weep. Get a pillow - cause you're going to sleep. (Light flash. Zap sound) There you go handsome... Sleeping handsome. I like the sound of that.

(Evil laughter)

MORGAN (CONT.)

I figured Prince Charles would cheat at his own game and not allow me to win the riddle contest. That's why I had the sleeping spell ready. And it's a very special sleeping spell that we have to let work over time. In time, the spell will be powerful enough for me to have my revenge.

(Laughs evilly... Sees someone enter. Becomes sweet and innocent)

Oh hello... I have no idea what happened to the prince... He said he was getting ever so sleepy and poof... He was off to dreamland. What? How could you think little old me did this? A witch? I'm not a witch. How could you say such a thing? A wand? Is that what this is? I thought it was a back scratcher. Okay. fine. You got me. Yes, I am a witch and it was no accident. But I'm afraid you won't be able to do anything about it.

(Points wand)

Only a little rest so I can do what's best.

(Zaps)

Just a short little sleep for you, only long enough to help my plan along. I'll wake him all right. I'll wake him with a magic kiss. One that will put him under my power.... Forever!

(Evil laughter)

END OF MONOLOGUE

SPIRIT OF CHRISTMAS INDIGESTION
monologue for female
From "Ebony Scrooge"
ISBN-13: 978-1537655239

(Ebony is sitting at a desk with cake, tea and paperwork. She has a pen in one hand and a teacup in the other)

EBONY

(Takes another bite of cake)

That Roberta has no work ethic, but she can sure bake a good cake.

(Yawns)

What kind of tea is this?

(Looks at label on tea bag)

Sleepy time?!

(Yawns)

That idiot.

(Eyes get heavy)

I have a mountain over paperwork to do.

(Drifts off)

I must get it done...

(Falls asleep on table. A thump in the kitchen wakes her)

What was that?

(Moves toward kitchen L)

EBONY (CONT.)

Roberta? Are you still here?

(Another thump)

Oh, my goodness. It could be a thief.

(Heavy steps. Takes out cell phone)

I better call the police.

(Hits phone)

Battery's dead? Stupid discount calling plan.

(More thumps. She picks up fork)

I've got a rather large weapon in here and I'm not afraid to use it.

(Hears rattling, moaning, and other spooky sounds. Drops fork)

Uh, was it the tea or the cake that's doing this to me? I swear I'm hearing...

(The ghost of MARLA appears L)

A... A... An Apparition

(Scared)

Go away. I know you're something I ate that I shouldn't have. I need some medicine. Some plop, plop, fizz, fizz, and you'll be gone. Begone foul spirit. I know you're only heartburn.

(Goes and sits)

The only warning I need is on the tea label. Now I'm seeing things.

(Grabs papers and yawns)

EBONY (CONT.)

Where was I before the spirit of Christmas indigestion appeared?

(Yawns and drifts off. Lights fade to black. Twelve strokes of the clock. And a ghostly sound is heard)

END OF MONOLOGUE

THE SUNDAY GAMBLE
monologue for male
from "Death of an Insurance Salesman"
ISBN-13: 978-1518665547

PARKER

Come on... Please. I'm begging you God. Give this to me and I will give you my all... I will dedicate myself to you. Scout's honor!

(Tries to figure out number of fingers for Scout salute)

I need this. I know I always pray that but this time I really do. I know it seems like I pray to you only when I really want something ... Or really worried about something. But that's what you're there for right? Like an exam in school or the flu. I know should talk to you when things are good. I know it's good to be thankful for good things too. I just forget. Forgive me? Forgive and forget? You forgive I forget. Just a little prayer humor. Sorry about that. So how about it God? I really need this. I have never wanted anything so much in my life. Please help my team to win on Sunday. I have a lot riding on this one. And if you give me this, I promise to be at church every Sunday... except this one. But every single Sunday after this. How is that for a deal?

END OF MONOLOGUE

SYMBOL OF THE REVOLUTION
monologue for female
from "A Hysterical History of the American Revolution"

(Kitty Greene is the wife of American Revolution General Greene and future co-inventor of the Cotton Gin. She is part of a fictional meeting of Revolutionary women)

KITTY

Thank you for inviting me to be part of this momentous meeting of the women of the American Revolution. Oh, this is so exciting. I move that we do some open act of protest. But nothing as messy as that awful tea party in Boston. Imagine dumping all that lovely tea in the harbor.

(Pauses to think)

Maybe we could burn our petticoats? Doesn't see a good reaction from the other women. No. That is way too 1760's. Thinks again. How about a symbol? We could rally behind a woman that symbolizes what we stand for! Ladies! I will present to you two symbols of the Women of the American Revolution.

(KITTY gets some props. She puts on a bonnet and holds up a water pitcher)

First, we have Molly Pitcher. She is the brave woman who ran pitchers of water to the canons to cool them during battle. When her husband fell under enemy fire, she took his post and fired the cannon!

(KITTY then rips off her bonnet and pulls out her hair so she has crazy hair and picks up a hatchet. She gets a crazy look in her eyes and swings the ax yelling a battle cry)

And we have Molly Hatchet... Yee-haw! I'm gonna git me a lobster back!

(KITTY realizes she has scared everyone and hides the ax behind her skirt)

Sorry to scare you, Mrs. Washington. I'll put away the ax now.

END OF MONOLOGUE

TAKE IT EASY

monologue for male

(female version from "Blondes Prefer Gentlemen")

ISBN-13: 978-1985331877

RANDY

You look nervous. You sure you're okay? Just take it easy. Breathe. Breathe. That's good. Don't think about the crowd okay? Think about… uh… think about that pretty dancer out there. Isn't she great? Maybe I can ask her to stand off to the side and you can just look at her instead of the audience. Or imagine the crowd in their underwear. They say that works sometimes. Or imagine that dancer in her underwear. Sorry. I'll stop talking about the dancer.

(Long pause)

I wonder if she's single. Sorry, sorry. Okay, I'll focus. What were talking about? Hey! Don't be mad. Where are you going?! You can't leave. You're on next! Come back here!

END OF MONOLOGUE

WAITING ON THE BRIDE
monologue for male
from "Flowers in the Desert"
ISBN-13: 978-1530169085

LINC

Where is she? The ceremony starts soon and she's not even here. I hope something didn't happen to her. The one time we don't go somewhere together and something happens. She's not calling or texting. That's not good. It might be bad. Really bad. I wonder if someone can find out if there are any accidents near here. I wish I hadn't picked that hotel for her across town. I should have looked harder for something closer to the church. This is terrible. I couldn't live with myself if something happened to her. I should have bought her a safer car. I didn't check the safety rating when we bought it. It's so small. What if some big truck...stop...don't think about it. Think about something else... The honeymoon... The honeymoon will be so nice... A week away with no one bugging us. What if she is late and we don't make the flight? What if she isn't coming at all? I know she loves me but I know this has all been so stressful ... Maybe it got to be too much for her... Does she really want to add all my baggage to her life? I wouldn't wish my problems on anyone. She's a pretty amazing person to put up with it all. But maybe it got to be too much when thought about being stuck with my problem... Stuck... Forever... Scary words... No wonder she ran away... I never wanted her to feel stuck... I wanted her to feel free... But she is like a beautiful song bird you have in your home but you decide it might be better for her if you let her go. You open the cage but she doesn't fly away... She stays with you singing her wonderful song, making every day more beautiful with her presence... Is she here? Thank you God she is here... I am getting married... I really am... Why am I so nervous... I can't wait to see her... She must be so beautiful today... I am a lucky guy... How did I get so lucky? I can't wait to spend the rest of my life with her. I'm so happy she wants that too.

END OF MONOLOGUE

WHERE'S MY PRINCE CHARMING?
monologue for female
from "The Ghosts of Detention"
ISBN-13: 978-1499111309

PRINCESS

Okay, people. I wished upon a star. I guess it does make a difference who I are! Do I have to be some poor nobody wannabe? Do I need some kind of kryptonite like a little pea? Did my prince get turned into a frog and he's now hiding in some creepy bog waiting for me to find him? I don't even know how to swim. What's the use of dreaming anymore. No one is beating down my door. I need to be some kind of damsel in distress to get some attention I guess. Where's my Prince Charming? Is there something about me that's alarming? All I get is Prince Pampered who spends his whole life hampered by being royally stuck up. Or there's Prince Never Grow Up who is way too pretty in his curls. All these boys make me want to hurl. Why can't I find a man sized prince who will sweep me off my feet and take me to far away lands. He will hold me with his strong hands and devote his life to me. Is that what I want? Is that what I dream about? If I don't get it, will I forever pout and cry because I didn't get my way? I just want to feel special. I want to feel like they care. I want them to bravely face any challenge for me. Enter my heart if you dare. Lock me in a tower. Make me your precious flower. I want you to battle your way against dragons to win my love today. Quit playing with your toys and prove your worth to me, boys. I promise I will be the perfect princess for you to please. I will be good to you and I won't be a tease... much. Who am I kidding? I'm chasing a dream. They say I got everything in life but it is nothing it seems. Where is my happy ending?!

END OF MONOLOGUE

WHO WANTS TO BE MY BULLY?
monologue for male
from "Bullied, Bungled and Botched"
ISBN-13: 978-1518661082

LUKE

Hello. I am taking applications to my official bully. I want to make sure the right person is picking on me day after day. It's a very unique and special relationship. Ready for some questions? Okay. First of all, are you interested in my lunch money or my lunch? Because if you need the cash I will bring that it if you prefer to have me bring a lunch already prepared, I can do that too. No, this isn't a joke. I'm very serious about this. Or do you prefer I tell jokes? Are you the knock knock joke kind where you walk up and knock on my head? Knock! Knock! Or do you prefer the walk in to the bar kind of jokes? I could try work up some dirty jokes too but that seems more appropriate for your friends to tell than your victims. We have to have the right kind of relationship here. We need familiarity without closeness. I can provide services such as homework preparation and go-foring - in return I ask that I only receive swirlies at the end of the day so I can go home and shower after. And then one more thing - the most important part of all this - I ask for your protection. I want you to protect me from all the other bullies. This has to be an exclusive bullying arrangement and you have to make sure you step in at the first sign of any danger from other bullies. I like my day to be predictable - deliver your homework in the morning - lunch or lunch money at noon and then a farewell swirly or wedgie in the afternoon - yes I will even throw a few wedgies in the deal - so what do you say? Do we have a deal? Good - sign here please.

END OF MONOLOGUE

"YAR!"
monologue for male

PIRATE KELLY

Avast there matey. It be Talk like a Pirate Day. Hand over those donuts. Donuts are always free on Talk like a Pirate Day. I be looking for the perfect donut. It has to be the perfect length… twice as big as me mouth.

Once I found the donut of me dreams and I have been on an endless search for one to match it's perfection. Let me tell ye a tale of the most delicious of donuts... but be warned… it's not for the faint of heart.

(PIRATE KELLY gets a dreamy look in his eye as he remembers eating the perfect donut)

Once was a donut ever so sweet
That its taste could never be beat
It was as heavenly as can be
Like it was made just for me
Better than a bottle of rum
After a few bites I felt undone
But it slipped from me grip
And that donut took a dip
Like a sinking ship lost at sea
Now food for fishes, bad for me

(The memory of losing the donut gets him crying. Then he looks around and realizes the person with the donuts is gone)

Where'd she go? You can't get rid of me that easy. I must have ye donuts!

(PIRATE KELLY runs off stage and after a moment he runs across again)

END OF MONOLOGUE

TIPS FOR NEW ACTORS ABOUT STAGE FRIGHT

The short monologues below are a good way to help you work through your stage fright if this is something you struggle with. By practicing short monologues, it can boost your confidence. Don't feel bad about being nervous. Some very famous people had stage fright: Elvis Presley, Barbra Streisand, Meryl Streep and Sir Laurence Olivier.

Stage fright is a challenge a lot of people have. I've acted many times but I still get nervous right before I go on. But once I start performing I totally forget about the people and focus on my character. Focus only on your character and your story. Become that character. If you become the character, then it is this other person up there and not yourself. If you need to face the audience, don't look at anyone. Pick a point to look at in the back of the room and focus on that. Many performers (including myself) use the nervous energy and put it in their performance.

Singer Stevie Nicks explains how this helps her performance rather than hurts it. "If you have stage fright, it never goes away. But then I wonder: is the key to that magical performance because of the fear?"

17704655R00043

Printed in Great Britain
by Amazon